THE TELESCOPE

THE
TELESCOPE

INVENTIONS THAT CHANGED OUR LIVES

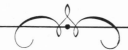

Lisa Yount

WALKER AND COMPANY New York

For my favorite stargazers:

Steve, Alec, and especially HARRY

Library of Congress Cataloging in Publication Data
Yount, Lisa.
  The telescope.

  (Inventions that changed our lives)
  Includes index.
  Summary: Describes how the telescope came to be invented, its effect on
scientific study, especially astronomy, and the impact it has had on our lives.
    1. Telescope—Juvenile literature. [1. Telescope]
I. Title.
QB88.Y68 1983 522'.2 82-23850
ISBN 0-8027-6492-4
ISBN 0-8027-6493-2 (lib. bdg.)

First published in the United States of America in 1983 by the Walker Publishing Company, Inc.

Published simultaneously in Canada by John Wiley & Sons Canada, Limited,
Rexdale, Ontario.

ISBN: 0-8027-6492-4 Trade
      0-8027-6493-2 Reinf.

Library of Congress Catalog Card Number: 82-23850

Printed in the United States of America

10 9 8 7 6 5 4 3 2 1

81-536   (1984-85)

CONTENTS

FOREWORD

ANCIENT PEOPLE regarded the sun, moon, planets, and stars as mysterious, but at the same time, they observed the heavenly bodies and learned a good deal about their positions and movements. This knowledge was the beginning of the science of astronomy. It helped them to find paths across the sea and to plant and harvest their crops at the right time of the year. However, they had little hope of finding out what these bodies were really like.

Almost 400 years ago, an invention called the telescope gave people new "eyes" to see the stars. The telescope made objects in the sky seem bigger and brighter. It revealed things that no one had seen before. Within a few years of its invention, the telescope had destroyed beliefs that people had held for thousands of years.

As time went on, people learned how to make bigger and better telescopes. Cameras and other devices helped telescopes make distant objects appear closer. Telescopes were invented that could "see" without using light. Finally, telescopes were sent into space.

Telescopes changed the way people thought about their world. Before the telescope was invented, most people believed that the Earth was at the center of the universe. Telescopes showed that the Earth was only a tiny dot in the immense reaches of space. Ancient people thought that the heavens were perfect and unchanging. Telescopes showed that the sky was a place of constant change.

Although telescopes destroyed forever the idea that human beings were at the center of the universe, they also showed that people could learn about anything, even the most far-off stars.

Largely because of the telescope, people began to think seriously about traveling into space. The astronauts who walked on the moon were following a path first shown by light falling through a telescope tube.

1

The First Telescopes

"I MADE THE WEATHER vane on that church tower jump over to me!" cried Hans Lippershey's apprentice.

The boy worked in Lippershey's spectacle shop in 1608 in the Dutch town of Middleburg. Lippershey had never seen him so excited.

The apprentice handed his master two round pieces of glass. "I did it with these," he explained.

Lippershey looked at the pieces with interest. One curved inward, like the bowl of a spoon. "Hold that one near your eye," the boy told him.

"Now hold this piece in your other hand and stretch out your arm." The apprentice pointed to the second piece of glass, which bulged out on both sides. "Look at the weather vane through both pieces."

Lippershey did as the boy told him. Suddenly the bird-shaped weather vane seemed to swell before his eyes. He found he could see every feather on its metal head. The apprentice was right!

This is the story most often told about the way the telescope was invented. Lippershey himself may have told it when he asked the Dutch government in 1608 for exclusive rights to make his "instrument for seeing far." The instrument was a metal tube with the two pieces of glass fastened in it.

Several other Dutchmen later claimed that they had made the same kind of device before Lippershey. Even if they had, Lippershey was the first person to tell the world about this amazing invention.

It was not surprising that the first telescope should appear in a spectacle maker's shop. Spectacles, or glasses, had been helping people see better for over 300 years before Lippershey's time. The shops where they were made had both of the shapes of glass needed for a simple telescope. Sooner or later someone was sure to combine the shapes in the right way.

The curved pieces of glass used in spectacles are called *lenses*. There are lenses in people's eyes, too, though of course they are not made of glass. Spectacle lenses are used to correct faults in the eye's lens.

A lens gathers light. Its curved shape bends light so that the light rays come to a point. A lens that curves outward is called *convex*. It makes things look blurry but larger than they really are. A lens that curves inward is *concave*. It makes things look clear but small. A combination of these two, held a proper space apart, can make things both larger and clearer. That is what Hans Lippershey and his apprentice found out.

A telescope helps a person's eye gather light. The more light the eye gathers, the better it can see things that are small, dim, or far away. In a way, a telescope makes the person's eye bigger. An astronomer looking through the 200-inch (5-meter) telescope at Mount Palomar is like a giant with an "eye" as wide as a swimming pool! That "eye" can gather 800,000 times more light than the astronomer's own eye.

Dutch government leaders were very interested in Hans Lippershey's invention. They hoped it would help them win the war they were fighting against Spain. It might let Dutch sailors spot far-off Spanish ships.

As a military secret, however, the telescope was a failure. Once people heard about it, they had no trouble figuring out how to make one. Telescopes began appearing all over Europe only a few months after Lippershey first showed off his invention.

One person who made his own telescope was an Italian mathematician named Galileo Galilei. Instead of using his "far-seeing glass" to look for ships, however, Galileo turned it toward the heavens. What he saw there changed the way people thought about the universe. In fact, Galileo's discoveries were so revolutionary that they nearly cost him his life.

People had studied the heavens for thousands of years before Galileo's time. They had learned a great deal. The ancient Greeks knew the size of the Earth and the distance between it and the moon. The Mayas of South America had an accurate calendar that

Two of the first telescopes, built in 1609 by Galileo.
David Wool.

stretched thousands of years into the past and future. Arabs and Europeans had invented instruments that could measure the positions of the stars very exactly. Still, most Europeans of Galileo's time believed that all heavenly bodies went around the Earth. This idea fit in with the notion that human beings were at the center of the universe.

This picture of the heavens was supported by the Bible as well as by writings of the philosophers of ancient Greece. Disagreeing with this belief meant going against the teachings of the Catholic Church—a crime called *heresy*. It could be punished with torture or death or both.

Still, some people dared to argue with the Church's beliefs about the heavens. One man who did so was a Polish scientist named Nicholas Copernicus. In 1543, just before his death, Copernicus published a book he had worked on for years. It stated that Earth and the other planets went around the sun. Copernicus had worked out this idea through mathematics.

Galileo was sure that Copernicus was right. When he turned his telescope to the night sky, he hoped to find things that would support Copernicus's view of the heavens.

Five planets other than Earth were known in Galileo's time. They were Mercury, Venus, Mars, Jupiter, and Saturn. These planets were called "wandering stars" because they did not follow the same path as most objects in the night sky. For the first time, using the telescope, Galileo saw the planets as round bodies,

Galileo demonstrating his telescope. *Yerkes Observatory.*

quite different from the stars.

One night when he looked through the telescope, Galileo saw three points of light near the planet Jupiter. When he looked again the next night, he found that the lights had changed position. Later, he saw a fourth light. It also seemed to be moving.

Galileo watched the four lights for many nights.

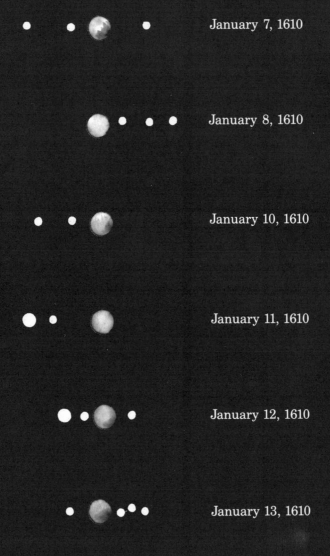

January 7, 1610

January 8, 1610

January 10, 1610

January 11, 1610

January 12, 1610

January 13, 1610

WHAT GALILEO SAW

Four small bodies circling Jupiter, as seen by Galileo.
David Wool.

They disappeared and reappeared. He decided that they were circling around Jupiter, just as the moon circles Earth. He knew that no one had ever seen these bodies before. With an instrument less powerful than a pair of modern binoculars, Galileo had discovered four new members of the solar system!

Galileo described his discoveries in a book called *The Starry Messenger*, published in 1610. The book caused a sensation. Many people admired it. Others were shocked. When Galileo tried to get doubters to see for themselves, some refused even to look through his telescope.

Galileo shocked even more people in 1613, when he began claiming that his discoveries supported the ideas of Copernicus. In 1616, Church officials warned Galileo not to write anything else that agreed with Copernicus. Galileo was not the type to let people tell him what to do, however. He went on making discoveries—and writing about them.

A Church court put Galileo on trial for heresy in 1633. It threatened him with torture unless he denied his beliefs. Galileo was a sick old man by then. He did as the court asked. He never really changed his mind, though.

The Church stopped Galileo, but it could not stop the spread of his ideas. More and more people tested these ideas by looking through telescopes themselves. Partly because of the telescope, people began to understand that using their senses, instead of relying on authorities, was the way to find out the truth.

2

Refractors
and Reflectors

THE FIRST MAN to improve on Galileo's telescope never looked through it. He was a German named Johannes Kepler. Kepler had studied the heavens before Galileo began using telescopes. He had used mathematics to figure out the paths that the planets followed around the sun.

Kepler had bad eyes. He admired Galileo's work, but he himself could see very little through a telescope. Instead of looking through telescopes, he tried to figure out how they worked.

Galileo's telescope, like Lippershey's, used one concave and one convex lens. Kepler decided that two different convex ones might work better.

Telescopes made with Kepler's design allowed people to see four times more sky at a time than Galileo's did. They showed things more clearly, too. They had one strange feature, however. Anything seen through them appeared to be upside down! Luckily, that was not important to people looking at moons and stars.

Both Galileo's and Kepler's telescopes used lenses. They bent or *refracted* light. Any telescope that uses lenses to gather light is called a *refractor*, or *refracting telescope*.

Early refractors had several problems. The shape of their lenses caused one problem. All the light rays gathered by a telescope must come together at a single point, the *focus*, in order to make a clear picture. The lenses in early refractors had surfaces shaped like parts of spheres. Light passing through different parts of such a lens came to a focus in different places. Because the light did not have a single focus, things seen through these telescopes looked blurry.

A Dutchman, Christian Huygens (HY-gunz), found one way around this trouble. He used lenses that bent light only a little. Unfortunately, the light came to a focus a long way behind the lens. This meant that Huygens's telescopes had to be very long, because the second, or eyepiece, lens had to be behind the focus of the first lens. One of Huygens's telescopes measured 123 feet (37 meters). Huygens had to place one lens of this telescope on top of a high pole. He tied the other lens to it with a long string.

Refracting telescopes also had a second problem. It had to do with color. White light is really made up of light of different colors. (You can see the colors of sunlight spread out in a rainbow.) A lens bends different colors of light by different amounts. Red light is bent

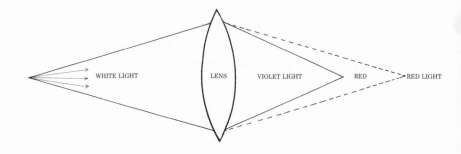

WHITE LIGHT · LENS · VIOLET LIGHT · RED · RED LIGHT

A lens bends the different colors of white light un-
equally. Red light (broken line) is bent least, violet is
bent most. *David Wool.*

least and comes to a focus farther from the lens than
violet light, which is bent the most. Because different
colors came to a focus at different places, rainbow
halos appeared around everything seen through early
refractors.

A Scottish astronomer named James Gregory described a cure for this color trouble in 1663. Seven
years later Sir Isaac Newton constructed a working
telescope based on Gregory's idea. (Newton was the
great British scientist who discovered the law of
gravity.)

The answer to the color problem was mirrors. Mirrors *reflect* light, or bounce it back, instead of bending
it. They reflect the light of all colors equally. Gregory
and Newton guessed that there would be no colored

halos in a mirror telescope. Such a telescope could also show clear pictures while remaining quite short. It would remove the need for pole-and-string giants like Huygens's.

Telescopes that use mirrors to gather light are

Isaac Newton's reflecting telescope, 1668. *David Wool.*

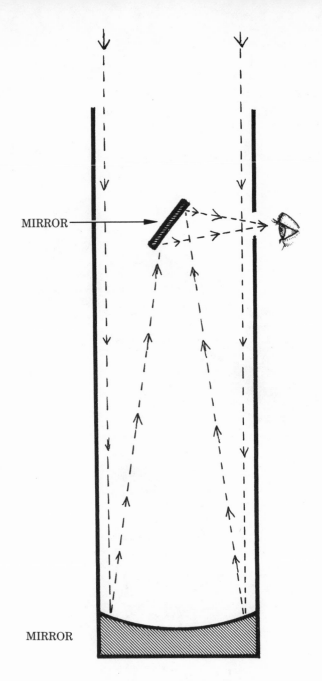

MIRROR

MIRROR

Diagram of Newton's telescope. *David Wool.*

called *reflectors*. Newton used a concave mirror instead of a refractor's convex lens. In his telescope rays of light pass straight down an open tube and strike a mirror at the bottom. This mirror reflects the light back up the tube to a small flat mirror. The small mirror is set at an angle and sends the light through an eyepiece lens in the side of the telescope.

Newton's reflector aroused great interest. People could not really see much with it, however. The first reflector good enough for astronomy was not made until 1721. That was more than fifty years after Newton's attempt.

The trouble with early reflectors was their mirrors. People did not make mirrors by coating glass with silver or aluminum, as they do now. Mirrors were made from shiny metals. Grinding and polishing the metals to the shape and smoothness needed for good telescope mirrors was almost impossible. The metals also tarnished easily. The mirrors had to be repolished and reshaped every time that happened.

Meanwhile, people finally learned to make lenses for refracting telescopes that did not show colored halos. An English father and son, John and Peter Dollond, began making the new lenses in 1758. Each lens was really a combination of two lenses, made of different kinds of glass. A convex lens of one kind of glass was placed against a concave lens of the other kind. The two lenses bent light in different ways. Each made up for the faults of the other.

Many astronomers liked the new refractors. Others, however, preferred reflectors, in spite of their hard-to-handle mirrors. One of those astronomers who favored reflectors was William Herschel.

Herschel, a British astronomer, looked through his first reflector in 1773. After that he spent every spare minute on astronomy. He could not afford to buy big telescopes, so he decided to make his own. His house became a telescope factory by day and an astronomical observatory by night.

Herschel even took on the demanding job of making his own mirrors. First he melted the mirror metal and poured it into a mold. Sometimes the mirror cracked as it cooled. Then he had to start over. When the mirror was cool, it had to be ground and polished. Herschel often worked at these tasks for hours at a time. His sister, Caroline, who later became an astronomer, read to him and even fed him as he worked. Once Herschel ground a mirror for sixteen hours without stopping.

In 1781, Herschel saw a puzzling "cloudy star" through a telescope in his garden. At first, Herschel thought it was a comet, but it didn't follow the kind of path he would expect a comet to take. Herschel finally accepted the unbelievable. The object had to be a new planet! This planet is now called Uranus.

Herschel also figured out that the sun was moving within our galaxy, the Milky Way. Galileo and other astronomers had shown that Earth was not too different from the other planets. Now Herschel showed that the sun acted much like other stars, which also

WILLIAM HERSCHEL. *Yerkes Observatory.*

William Herschel's 40-foot telescope. *Yerkes Observatory.*

move through space. The human world was becoming a small speck in an ever larger universe.

During this time telescopes grew bigger and bigger. Herschel was the first to figure out exactly why big telescopes were better than small ones. Big mirrors had more surface area, so they could gather more light. They made things seen through them look brighter. With a big telescope an astronomer could see more stars than with a small one.

Herschel's skill and patience let him make larger reflectors than anyone else ever had. His biggest one had a mirror 48 inches (1.2 meters) across. It was set in a tube 40 feet (12.2 meters) long.

Even this giant, however, was outdone by a reflector made in the next century. William Parsons, the Earl of Rosse, built it on his estate in Ireland. When Rosse's huge telescope was finished in 1845, it rose 56 feet (17 meters) into the air. Its main mirror was 72 inches (1.8 meters) across. Rosse, like Herschel, made the mirror himself.

"The Leviathan of Parsonstown" was a great tourist attraction, but its size made it hard to move. It was in a poor location, under skies that were almost always cloudy. Even with its huge mirror, it did not see things as well as many small refractors then being made.

Refractors and reflectors are no longer rivals, as they were in their early history. They are now both recognized as being valuable, but for different reasons. Refractors are better for studying planets and other

nearby objects. Large reflectors, however, are better for seeing far-off stars. Both kinds of telescopes are widely used today.

The Leviathan of Parsonstown. *Yerkes Observatory.*

3

Improvements

IF YOU ASKED a professional astronomer what it feels like to look through a big telescope, he or she might answer, "I don't know." Strange as it seems, astronomers in observatories seldom look through telescopes anymore. They let cameras and other devices do their looking for them.

It is easy to see why cameras began being used with telescopes soon after photography was invented. Once you stop looking at something, your eye's picture of it is gone. You cannot remember the thing exactly as you saw it and you cannot show it to someone else. A photograph, on the other hand, can be kept for study. Many people can use it, and it will look the same to all of them.

Cameras have other advantages, too. A photographic plate can be left in place for minutes or hours as a telescope follows a group of stars across the sky. The longer a plate is exposed, the more light it gathers. It will show more and more dim stars. (This can't go on forever, though. Light from bright stars and the "airglow," or night-sky light, finally drown out the light of dim stars.)

Photography was invented in 1826. John W. Draper, an American, took the first astronomical photograph 14 years later. It was a picture of the moon. Draper's telescope had a clockwork device that let it follow the moon across the sky. Draper got a clear picture after 20 minutes. By 1852 new developments in photography made it possible to take a picture of the moon in 20 seconds instead of 20 minutes.

Telescopes, cameras, and other new inventions worked hand in hand. Photographs made far better sky maps than drawings did. A photometer, an instrument used to measure light, could measure the brightness of stars in photographs. Another machine compared pictures of the same part of the sky taken at different times. If a star moved against the background, it seemed to "jump" from picture to picture. Very small movements could be spotted in this way.

The marriage of telescope and camera was not ideal, however. Gathering enough light to take a picture of a faint star could still take hours. During all that time the telescope had to move smoothly and carefully to track the star. Otherwise the picture would blur.

Another problem was that only the center of a large telescope's field of view was useful for picture-taking. Images near the edges of the field were mis-shapen.

A European astronomer named Bernhardt Schmidt found a cure for this trouble. In the late 1920s, Schmidt made a new kind of telescope. It combined a mirror and a specially shaped lens. The lens corrected certain faults in the mirror that affected photography. The result was a telescope that provided a very wide field of view in each picture.

Many observatories now have big Schmidt telescopes. A large part of the sky can be studied at once with such a telescope. Some Schmidt telescopes can get a million stars into a single picture.

Other devices, such as TV-like cameras and computers, can be used with telescopes. Computers improve, or enhance, images. For example, they can block out the light of bright stars. Then dim stars will show more clearly.

Computer processing has made some unbelievable pictures. One such was taken at Kitt Peak National Observatory in Arizona. It looks like a picture of the sun. The big disc in the picture, however, is a giant star called Betelgeuse. Betelgeuse is so far away that its light, traveling at 186,000 miles (298,000 kilometers) a second, takes 520 years to reach Earth. Yet the picture even shows hot and cool patches on the star's surface!

Another aid for telescope "eyes" is called the *spectroscope*. It was invented by a German, Joseph von Fraunhofer (FRON–hoh–fur), around 1814.

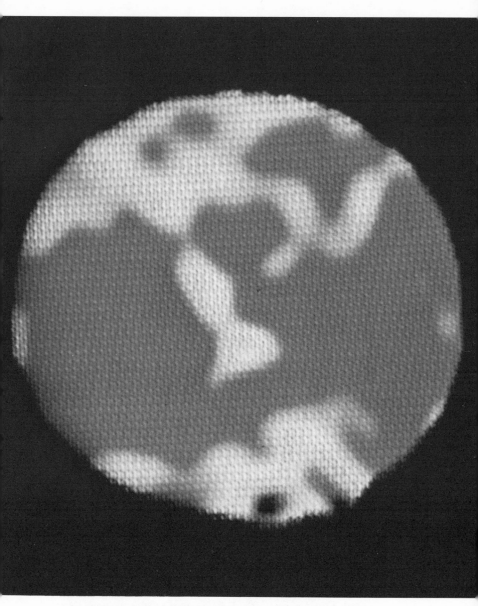

Computer-enhanced photograph of a giant star, Betelgeuse, showing hot and cool patches on the star's surface. *Kitt Peak National Observatory.*

Joseph von Fraunhofer demonstrating the spectroscope. *Yerkes Observatory.*

Like other scientists before him, such as Newton, Fraunhofer knew that white light could be broken into a rainbow, or *spectrum*, by passing the light through a triangular piece of glass called a *prism*. Earlier scientists had let light come through a small hole before it went through the prism. Fraunhofer, however, sent the light through a vertical slit instead. As a result, his rainbow came out as a row of colored lines.

At first sunlight seemed to make a continuous row of different colors. As Fraunhofer studied the light more closely, however, he found that he could see dark lines in the bright rainbow. To study the lines better, he added a small telescope to his slit and prism. The telescope helped to concentrate light on the slit. Fraunhofer called his invention a *spectroscope*.

Fraunhofer found that the light of some stars showed the same pattern of lines that the sun's light did. Other stars had dark lines in different places. This finding proved that the lines were more than a simple trick of the Earth's atmosphere and suggested that stars do in fact differ from each other in ways that the spectroscope could show.

Light from the gas flame of a lamp also made a rainbow in the spectroscope, Fraunhofer noticed. In this case, however, he saw bright lines against a dark background. Some of these lines were in the same places as the dark lines in the sunlight spectrum.

Later scientists found that different kinds of burning gas showed different *spectra* (plural of spectrum). In 1859, Robert Wilhelm Bunsen and Gustav

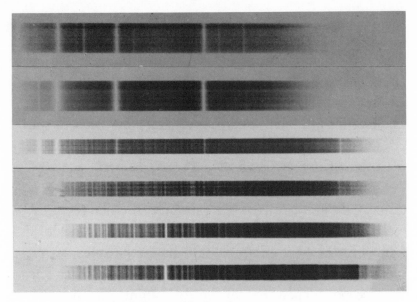

Spectra of different kinds of stars. *Yerkes Observatory.*

Kirchhoff showed that each chemical element had its own spectrum. The spectrum was like the element's fingerprint. By looking at a gas's spectrum, a trained person could find out what elements were in the gas.

Kirchhoff showed that the dark lines in the sunlight spectrum meant the same thing as the bright lines in the gas spectra. The spectra of the sun and stars could be "read" like those of gases on Earth. This meant that spectroscopes could show what stars were made of! Scientists could study heavenly bodies almost the way they studied chemicals in laboratories.

Spectroscopes led to many discoveries. They

helped scientists find a new chemical element, helium, in the sun 27 years before it was found on Earth. They showed how stars were different from each other. They helped astronomers figure out the pattern of changes that each star went through during its "life." They showed some of the strange things that happened to atoms in the hot centers of stars.

Today, spectroscopes are part of most large telescopes. Cameras take pictures of spectra. Computers also help to study these "star rainbows." Like cameras, spectroscopes joined telescopes to open a whole new world.

4

The Giants

LORD ROSSE'S LEVIATHAN seemed to mark the end of giant telescopes. They had proved hard to make and even harder to use. But then cameras and spectroscopes gave astronomers greater reason than ever to want more light. In the 1890s, a new generation of giant telescopes began to appear.

The new giants were made and used in ways that Rosse could never have dreamed of. They were also built in a place that would have surprised him: the United States. Before this, almost all important telescopes had been made in Europe. Now, however, Americans entered the field.

Most of the new giants eyed the stars from mountaintops in the American Southwest. Such clear, dry spots were a great improvement over the Leviathan's rainy Irish home. They also raised telescopes above the growing pollution of city air and the glare of city lights.

Almost all the American giants could be traced back to one man. He was a Chicagoan named George Ellery Hale. Hale was a fine astronomer and inventor. He was also a genius at making others share his enthusiasm—especially if they were rich people who might be willing to pay for observatories and telescopes.

The first man to come under Hale's spell was Charles T. Yerkes, a Chicago railroad tycoon. Hale talked Yerkes into giving money for building, first a telescope, then a whole observatory. Yerkes Observatory opened in 1897. It is at Williams Bay, on Lake Geneva, Wisconsin. It is the only home of a giant telescope that is not on a mountaintop.

Yerkes Observatory has the largest refracting telescope in the world. Its lens was made by Alvan Clark and Sons, an American company that was probably the world's finest lensmaker at the time. The lens is 40 inches (102 centimeters) across.

All the later American giants were reflectors. There were good reasons why no one tried to beat the Yerkes refractor's record. Even today it is hard to make large pieces of glass pure enough to be good telescope lenses. Also, a big lens is thick. It absorbs much of the light it gathers. It is heavy, too. A telescope lens can be supported only at the edges. A lens bigger than the Yerkes lens would sag in the middle.

New giant reflectors were possible because mir-

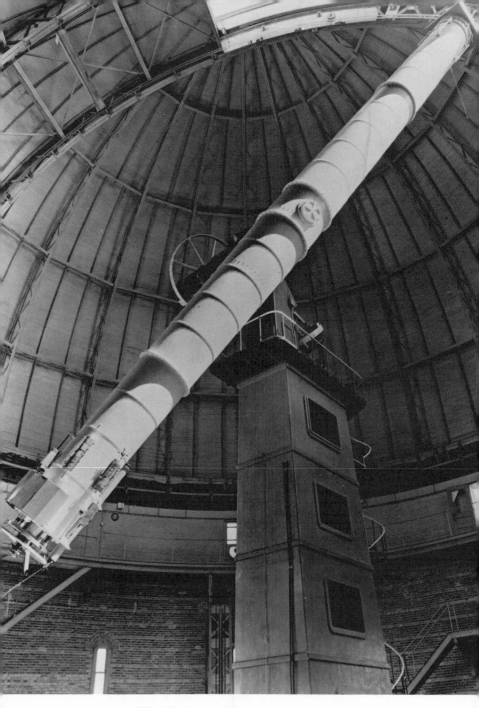

The Yerkes refractor. *Yerkes Observatory.*

ror-making had come a long way since the days of Herschel and Rosse. People no longer made mirrors from metal. Instead, they used glass coated with a thin, smooth film of silver. The first silvered telescope mirror was made in 1857.

Silvered glass mirrors were much easier to make than metal ones. They tarnished less easily, too. When a mirror did discolor, its silver coating could be replaced without reshaping the mirror. It was no wonder that when George Hale began planning another giant to follow the Yerkes telescope, he thought of mirrors rather than lenses.

He also thought of mountaintops. One mountaintop observatory, Lick Observatory, already existed in northern California. Hale chose a southern California peak, Mount Wilson.

Hale built big reflectors on Mount Wilson. The largest was called the Hooker telescope, after the man who paid for it. It had a mirror 100 inches (2.5 meters) across. This was the first telescope larger than Rosse's Leviathan. It was also far better in quality.

By the 1930s, observations from Mount Wilson were suffering badly from the smog and lights of the growing city of Los Angeles, which was nearby. Hale's last and finest telescope, therefore, was built on a more distant mountain, Mount Palomar. Hale didn't live to see this telescope's completion, but it is named after him. Its mirror is 200 inches (5 meters) across. For many years it was the largest telescope in the world.

Making the giant mirror for the Hale telescope

was a challenge greater than anything telescope makers had faced before. Corning Glass Works in New York took on the first part of the job. They made the mirror from a special kind of glass that resists heat. This glass does not change shape when the temperature changes, as ordinary glass does. Even tiny changes in shape can make a telescope mirror useless.

In 1934, Corning workers poured 21 tons of melted glass into a huge mold. The mold was made to give the back of the mirror a partly hollow, honeycomb shape. This shape would make the mirror less heavy.

Next the poured glass had to be cooled very slowly—less than 1°C. a day. Any sudden change in temperature might crack or warp the mirror. The cooling took 10 months.

In 1936 the huge piece of glass was carried slowly across the country in a special railroad car. Then workers at the California Institute of Technology began shaping and polishing it. That job took 11 years.

The finished mirror was given a coating of aluminum, which reflects light even better than silver does. It was set in a telescope with mounting and control motors so precise that the whole giant bulk could be moved smoothly a fraction of an inch at a time. The Hale telescope was finally dedicated in 1948.

The Hooker and Hale telescopes helped people to

Galaxies seen through the Hooker Telescope. *Yerkes Observatory.*

get an idea of how big the universe really is. They showed more and more far-off galaxies—huge star systems like our own Milky Way. Some are so far away that light from them has been traveling billions of years to reach us.

The giant telescopes are also time machines. Because light takes time to travel, looking far into space also means looking far into the past. In fact, the giant telescopes have helped people make guesses about the very beginning of the universe.

Certain changes in the spectra of far-off galaxies seem to mean that the galaxies are rushing away from each other. The universe appears to be expanding, or growing larger. Astronomers have guessed that the universe began with a huge explosion that they call the "Big Bang," and that the speeding galaxies are left over from that explosion.

For a long time the Hale telescope was the biggest reflector in the world. It has now been surpassed, however, by a giant reflector that was finished in Russia in 1976. The mirror for the Russian telescope is 236 inches (6 meters) across.

A different kind of giant is at Kitt Peak National Observatory, near Tucson, Arizona. Here a strange-looking triangular building houses the McMath telescope, the largest solar telescope in the world.

The McMath building towers 110 feet (34 meters)

The Hale Telescope. *Mt. Wilson and Palomar Observatories.*

into the air. Even so, two-thirds of it is below ground. The building's slanted arm holds a telescope 300 feet (91 meters) long. This telescope can show a picture of the sun almost 3 feet (76 centimeters) across.

Kitt Peak is the home of many other telescopes as well. In fact, it has the largest collection of working telescopes in the world. One, the Mayall telescope, is a reflector almost as big as the Palomar and Russian giants.

The Hale telescope and other giant reflectors seemed to represent the greatest size and power that light-gathering telescopes could reach. To learn still more about the universe, astronomers turned to new kinds of telescopes that did not use light at all.

The McMath Solar Telescope. *Kitt Peak National Observatory.*

5

The Radio Telescope

THERE'S MORE TO A RAINBOW than meets the eye.

What we call light is really particles of energy that move in waves. You see waves of different lengths as different colors. The waves in blue light are short. Waves in red light are longer.

Some energy waves are shorter than blue light or longer than red. All these waves are part of a spectrum much larger than that of visible light. Scientists call it the electromagnetic spectrum.

Stars, dust clouds, and other objects in space send out many kinds of energy besides light. During the last 50 years, astronomers have learned to make telescopes that gather these different kinds of energy. One of these new telescopes is the radio telescope.

The man who built the first radio telescope was not trying to learn about the stars. He was just doing his job. His name was Karl Jansky, and he worked for Bell

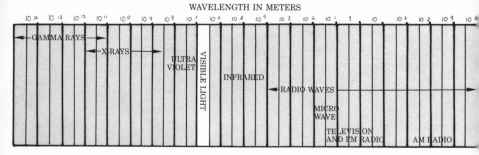

The electromagnetic spectrum. *David Wool.*

Telephone Laboratories in the early 1930s. Jansky's job was to find out what caused noises that sometimes interfered with messages sent by radiotelephone.

To look for the mystery signals, Jansky built a contraption that looked like something made from an overgrown Tinker Toy set. Most of it was an antenna that could pick up short radio waves. Jansky mounted the antenna on four old car wheels and placed it on a circular track. By moving it on the track, he could point it in different directions. He attached the antenna to a receiver that could record radio signals and measure their intensity.

Jansky found that some of the interference came from lightning. The rest, however, was made by a hissing noise that he could not explain. At first he thought it came from the sun. Then he realized it was coming from the center of the Milky Way. Jansky was getting radio "messages" from the stars!

This news didn't help Bell Laboratories much. Jansky's bosses sighed and set him to work on something else.

The only man who seemed much interested in Jansky's findings was named Grote Reber. Reber was a radio engineer and an amateur astronomer. He wanted to hear Jansky's strange signals for himself. In his backyard in Wheaton, Illinois, Reber built the first radio telescope that was really intended to be a radio telescope.

Reber's telescope had a big antenna shaped like a soup bowl. This was a lot like the shape of the big mirror in a reflecting telescope. The antenna gathered radio waves and brought them to a focus, much as the mirror in a reflecting telescope gathers and focuses light

Reconstruction of Karl Jansky's radio telescope. *National Radio Astronomy Observatory.*

Radio Telescope in Green Bank, West Virginia, with a wire mesh antenna 300 feet across. *National Radio Astronomy Observatory.*

waves. The antenna focused the radio waves on an aerial. The aerial sent the waves to a receiver, which turned them into electricity. The electric signals could be recorded and studied.

Later radio telescopes worked much the same way. They showed things about the heavens that light-gathering telescopes could not show. Some stars send out very little light but a good deal of radio energy, for example. These dim stars are hard to spot with light-gathering telescopes, but they can be found and studied easily with radio telescopes.

World War II interrupted the growth of the new science of radio astronomy. "Steerable dishes"—some-

The Very Large Array telescope at Socorro, New Mexico. *National Radio Astronomy Observatory.*

work in the daytime and under cloudy skies. They did not have to build their dishes on mountains. On the other hand, radio waves are weak. They are also much longer than light waves. For these reasons, a radio dish has to be much larger than a light-gathering telescope to pick up the same amount of information.

Fortunately, radio astronomers found ways to make several small dishes act like one big one. One way is to combine information from a pair of dishes far apart. Each dish in the pair makes a recording from the same part of the sky at exactly the same time. (Atomic clocks now synchronize the dishes. These clocks can keep time accurate to trillionths of a second.) Later the two recordings are compared. The result is like one recording made by a dish as wide as the distance between the two real dishes.

thing like Reber's—bloomed everywhere after the war, however. The largest is at Jodrell Bank, England. It is 250 feet (76 meters) across.

A radio telescope can be even larger than the one at Jodrell Bank, if it does not have to be moved. The world's largest nonsteerable dish is 1000 feet (305 meters) wide. This amazing structure is built in a bowl-shaped valley in Arecibo, Puerto Rico. It is covered with 39,000 aluminum sheets. Its surface is larger than the combined collecting surfaces of all the telescopes ever built.

Radio astronomers had certain advantages over people using light-gathering telescopes. They could

The Arecibo radio telescope in Puerto Rico. *National Astronomy and Ionosphere Center.*

A group of dishes called an *array* can make one big dish out of a number of smaller ones. The dishes in an array are fairly close together. All send their information to a single receiving set. Computers combine their parts of the radio picture to make a whole. The "dish" made by an array is as wide as the array is.

One radio telescope array dwarfs all others. It is called the Very Large Array (VLA). The VLA lies in a flat, dry plain near Socorro, New Mexico. It was finished in 1980.

Twenty-seven radio dishes make up the Y-shaped VLA. Each dish is 85 feet (26 meters) wide. Two of the Y's arms are 13 miles (21 kilometers) long. The third is only a little shorter. The dishes can be steered or aimed in different directions. They also can be carried to different parts of the array on railroad tracks. The VLA can "see" radio waves as sensitively as the Hale telescope sees light.

The universe revealed by radio telescopes is a violent place. Some powerful sources of radio waves seem to be colliding galaxies. Others are clouds of gas left by exploding stars.

Some of the strongest radio sources are called *quasars* (KWAY–sahrz). They send out great amounts of light, X-rays, and other energy as well as radio waves. No one knows exactly what quasars are or how they get their power.

Quasars are farther away than just about anything else earthly telescopes can pick up. What's more, they seem to be rushing away from us at almost the

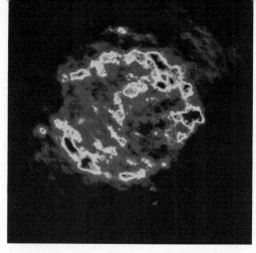

Radio map of the supernova remnant of a stellar explosion in the constellation Cassiopeia. *National Radio Astronomy Observatory.*

speed of light. Astronomers guess that they may have been formed fairly near the time of the Big Bang. If we could see quasars far enough away, perhaps we might see the beginning of the universe.

The only waves besides radio and light waves that can be studied much on Earth are infrared (in-
-fruh–RED) waves. You can feel nearby infrared waves as heat. Telescopes that pick up infrared waves from space have to have special cooling systems. Several such telescopes have been built in Hawaii. They are on top of a dead volcano called Mauna Kea.

Among other things, infrared telescopes tell us about the birth of stars. Newborn stars are too cool to give off light. Clouds of gas hide them. Their infrared waves, however, show that they are there.

The Earth's atmosphere blocks out ultraviolet waves, X-rays, and most other waves in the electromagnetic spectrum. Astronomers could begin to study these waves only when telescopes could be sent above the atmosphere. This first happened in the late 1950s, when the age of space astronomy began.

6

The Future
of Telescopes

Do OTHER STARS have planets? If so, are intelligent beings living on them? Where do quasars get their energy? How did the universe begin? When and how will it end?

Telescopes built in the next 20 years may help us answer those questions. They will also help us answer questions we don't yet know enough to ask.

Some of the new telescopes will be on Earth. Others will do their work in space. They will be like telescopes of the past in some ways. In other ways, they will be as different as the Hale telescope was from Rosse's Leviathan.

To find out more about far-off objects such as quasars, astronomers on Earth need light-gathering telescopes very much bigger than the ones they have now. Even if a solid mirror for such a big telescope could be made, it would be too heavy and too costly to be practical. Therefore, new giants will have to be made from small mirrors or mirror pieces working together. The designers of these "new technology telescopes" have learned much from the makers of radio telescopes.

Computers make it possible to build a giant telescope from small pieces. They can keep the different parts of the giant lined up exactly. They can move the mirrors separately up and down and from side to side, and to different degrees at the same time.

The first of the new giants is already at work. It is called the Multiple Mirror Telescope (MMT). The MMT is on Mount Hopkins, Arizona. It was finished in 1979.

The MMT has six mirrors set in one openwork metal frame. Each mirror is 72 inches (1.8 meters) across. Working together, the mirrors can gather as much light as a single mirror 176 inches (4.5 meters) across. In effect, the MMT is the third largest light-gathering telescope in the world. Yet it cost only ⅓ the price of a single-mirror telescope of the same size.

Some future giants will be bigger versions of the MMT. One "new technology telescope" planned by astronomers at Kitt Peak will have six separate mirrors. The mirrors will work together to make a single picture, as those of the MMT do. Each mirror will be 236 inches (6 meters) across—bigger than the Hale telescope mirror. The six together will make up one "giant mirror" 590 inches (15 meters) across.

Another kind of "new technology telescope" will

Multiple Mirror Telescope. *MMTO Observatory.*

have one giant mirror made of many small, six-sided parts. The big mirror will look something like a silver tile floor. A computer can make each "tile" move separately.

All the new giants are designed to save money and weight. Planners have found that several small mirrors cost less to build than one large one. They also weigh less. Making mirrors very thin is a second way to save weight. A third is to use the mostly hollow "honeycomb" or "egg crate" structure first used in the Hale telescope mirror. The MMT mirrors have this kind of design.

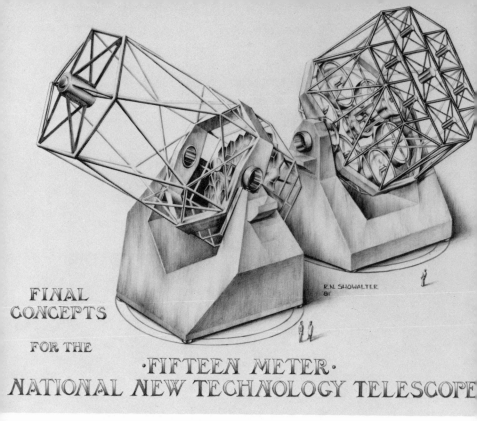

FINAL CONCEPTS FOR THE

·FIFTEEN METER·
NATIONAL NEW TECHNOLOGY TELESCOPE

R.N. SHOWALTER
81

New technology telescopes. *Kitt Peak National Observatory.*

Even the biggest of the new giants face certain problems. They lie at the bottom of an ocean of air that is full of dust and dirt. The air blocks out most energy waves from space, and its motion distorts light. The only way to escape these troubles is to send telescopes into space.

Telescopes were first lifted to the top of the atmosphere in balloons and rockets. A telescope in a rocket picked up ultraviolet waves from the stars in 1956, for example. A telescope camera in a balloon took fine pictures of the sun in 1957. Powerful X-ray sources were found in the sky by a rocket telescope in 1962.

The age of space astronomy began after Russia sent up the first artificial satellite in 1957. Later Russian and American satellites carried telescopes that picked up ultraviolet rays, X-rays, or gamma rays. Some satellites were whole orbiting observatories. One had 11 different telescopes. Satellites will continue doing important work for the science of astronomy.

Telescopes and cameras in space probes gave people their first close-up looks at the moon and planets. A Russian probe showed the back of the moon in 1959. Voyager probes took amazing pictures of Jupiter and Saturn in 1979 and 1980.

When people went into space, they took telescopes with them. Astronauts in Skylab, for example, took pictures of the sun that never could have been taken from Earth.

More work will be done with space telescopes in the future. The Space Telescope (ST) is scheduled to be carried into orbit by the space shuttle in 1985. It will do many kinds of astronomical work. Its mirror will be 96 inches (2.4 meters) across. That is not very big, as telescope mirrors go. However, because the ST will be in space, it will be able to see things that are 50 times fainter than the dimmest objects the Hale telescope can pick up.

The mirror for the Space Telescope has already been finished. People at Corning Glass Works made the glass for the mirror, as they did for the Hale tele-

scope. Computer-controlled polishing at the Perkin-Elmer Corporation gave the mirror an almost completely perfect surface.

Other kinds of telescopes may be used in space later on. Shuttle crews may assemble an array of light or radio telescopes in orbit. Radio dishes on the moon could be paired with others on Earth. Telescopes as large as the "new technology" giants being planned for Earth could be built in space.

Space telescopes will not replace Earth-based ones, however. The big telescopes on Earth are already built, or soon will be. Really large space telescopes, on the other hand, are not likely to be ready for many years. At present, telescopes on Earth last longer than those in space, and are cheaper to make.

Space telescopes and telescopes on Earth will work together. Cooperation is the key to today's astronomy—and tomorrow's. Groups of universities plan, build, and pay for the "new technology" giants. Scientists in different countries cooperate on long-range projects. Light, radio, and other telescopes provide different kinds of information that can be brought together and studied.

One project on which several kinds of telescopes might work together is the search for life in other star systems. Light-gathering giants in space can look for planets belonging to other stars. Infrared telescopes

The Space Telescope.
Courtesy Perkin-Elmer.

can pick out chemicals in space or on other planets that are like chemicals on Earth. Radio "ears" can listen for signals that might be sent by intelligent beings.

Since Galileo first looked at the sky, each new kind of telescope has led to important discoveries about the heavens. Each has changed the way people thought about their world.

As we bring our telescopes closer to the stars, who knows what wonders they will see? Many astronomers feel that this is the most exciting time for their science since Galileo's day.

As our telescopes improve and we venture farther and farther into space, our knowledge about the universe can only grow.

AFTERWORD

YOU, TOO, can turn your eyes to the stars. Perhaps you will want to become an *amateur* astronomer—someone who studies the skies as a hobby. Amateurs have made important discoveries. William Herschel, George Hale, and many other great astronomers began as amateurs.

You might start by using books and star maps to learn about the sky in your area. Then go outside and study the stars for yourself. See how many *constellations* (groups of stars that seem to make a picture) you can pick out.

Next, try to get a chance to look through a telescope. Even binoculars can show you the same wonders Galileo saw. Perhaps a family friend has a small telescope you can borrow. Perhaps you can use one belonging to an amateur astronomy club or an astronomy class at a nearby high school or college. Later on, you might buy a used telescope. You might even make a small telescope of your own. NEVER look at the sun with a regular telescope. You can ruin your eyes for life if you do.

Listed below are some books that can help you learn more about astronomy and telescopes.

Asimov, Isaac. *How Did We Find Out About the Universe?* New York: Walker Publishing Co., 1982.

Asimov, Isaac. *How Did We Find Out About Black Holes?* New York: Walker Publishing Co., 1978.

Berger, Melvin. *Quasars, Pulsars, and Black Holes in Space.* New York: G. P. Putnam's Sons, 1977.

Branley, Franklyn M. *The Nine Planets.* New York: Thomas Y. Crowell Co., 1978.

Knight, David C. *Galaxies: Islands in Space.* New York: William Morrow & Co., 1979.

Moore, Patrick. *The Young Astronomer and His Telescope.* New York: Orbiting Books, 1974.

Simon, Seymour. *Look to the Night Sky: An Introduction to Star Watching.* New York: The Viking Press, 1977.

You may also find the magazine *Odyssey* interesting. It is a magazine about astronomy and is written for young people.

Index

DAT

1-
10

522   Yount, Lisa
YOU   The telescope

DATE DUE	BORROWER'S NAME	
1-3-85	Bruce Keller	
11-25-87	Craig Gahin	

522   Yount, Lisa
YOU   The telescope